STEM Projects in **MINECRAFT**®

The Unofficial Guide to
MINECRAFT®
Physics

JILL KEPPELER

PowerKiDS
press

Published in 2025 by The Rosen Publishing Group, Inc.
2544 Clinton Street, Buffalo, NY 14224

First Edition

Editor: Greg Roza
Book Design: Rachel Rising
Illustrator: Matias Lapegüe

Photo Credits: Cover, pp. 1–24 Soloma/Shutterstock.com; pp. 4, 6, 8, 10, 12, 14, 16, 18, 20 Levent Konuk/Shutterstock.com; p. 5 Georgii Bychkovskii/Shutterstock.com; p. 13 Maui Topical Images/Shutterstock.com; p. 15 Romolo Tavani/Shutterstock.com.

Library of Congress Cataloging-in-Publication Data

Names: Keppeler, Jill, author.
Title: The unofficial guide to Minecraft physics / Jill Keppeler.
Description: Buffalo, NY : PowerKids Press, 2024. | Series: STEM projects
  in Minecraft | Includes index.
Identifiers: LCCN 2024001861 (print) | LCCN 2024001862 (ebook) | ISBN
  9781499446999 (library binding) | ISBN 9781499446982 (paperback) | ISBN
  9781499447002 (ebook)
Subjects: LCSH: Minecraft (Game)–Juvenile literature. | Physics–Juvenile
  literature.
Classification: LCC GV1469.35.M535 K464 2024 (print) | LCC GV1469.35.M535
  (ebook) | DDC 794.8/5–dc23/eng/20240130
LC record available at https://lccn.loc.gov/2024001861
LC ebook record available at https://lccn.loc.gov/2024001862

Manufactured in the United States of America

Some of the images in this book illustrate individuals who are models. The depictions do not imply actual situations or events.

CPSIA Compliance Information: Batch #CSPK25. For further information contact Rosen Publishing at 1-800-237-9932.

Find us on

Contents

A Branch of Science 4

Falling Down 6

Go with the Flow 10

In Motion 14

Ways to Move 16

Light and Heat 18

Redstone Power 20

Glossary 22

For More Information 23

Websites 24

A Branch of Science

Minecraft can teach you a lot about the real world, but the game's physics aren't quite like real-world physics. Physics is the study of matter, energy, force, and motion and the relationship among them. It's a major branch of science. Changing its rules in *Minecraft* can change many things. This can be an interesting thing to study!

If you play *Minecraft*, you've probably noticed how some things, like gravity, work in different ways. Knowing how they work can help you build and plan things. **Fluids** and other things may move differently. It's good to understand these things.

MINECRAFT MANIA

Fluids in *Minecraft* include water and **lava**. It's important to understand them, because you can drown in water and lava can burn you...and other things!

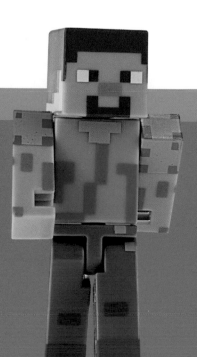

Waterfalls in *Minecraft* and the real world can be beautiful pieces of scenery!

5

Falling Down

Gravity is the force that pulls objects toward the center of Earth. It's why if you jump in the air, you'll fall back down to the ground. Gravity also gives things weight. Weight measures the force of gravity on an object.

Gravity is one of the biggest differences you'll notice between the real world and *Minecraft*. A *Minecraft* world is made mostly of blocks. Most of these blocks aren't affected by gravity. For example, if you build a tower out of blocks of stone, then take the lower blocks out, the higher ones will continue to float in the air.

MINECRAFT MANIA

The different physics in *Minecraft* means you can build some amazing things (like bridges or huge buildings) without having to think about how gravity will affect your creation.

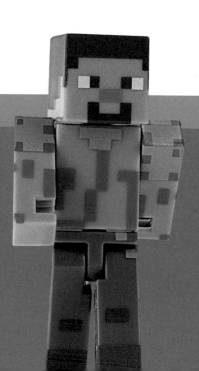

There would be many physical concerns to building a tall, thin structure like this in the real world. In *Minecraft*, you don't have to worry about them!

Still, some blocks in *Minecraft* do react to gravity. These include sand, red sand, gravel, concrete powder, **anvils**, snow layers (in some games), **scaffolding**, suspicious sand and gravel, and pointed dripstone. This means that if they don't have some sort of support under them, they fall!

Some of these blocks will **generate** naturally in a *Minecraft* world. When that happens, they may have nothing underneath them, but they'll stay still unless a mob or player **disturbs** one. This can make other blocks around them fall. Be careful, or you could end up buried in gravel or plunging into a pool of deep water!

MINECRAFT MANIA

Pointed dripstone generates in caves. It makes up pointed stalactites (which point downward) and stalagmites (which point upward). If a block supporting a stalactite breaks, it will fall.

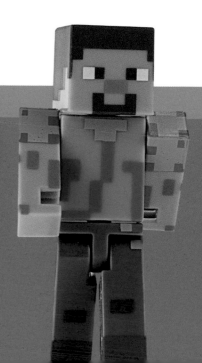

Beaches like this one can have pools of water with sand over them. If you disturb one block, the rest could fall into the water. You could fall with them!

Go with the Flow

Minecraft lava and water are affected by gravity too, but in a different way. They will both flow downward and around other things if there's a source block for them. They can't flow upward. Fluids that are moving will push on some other things to move in the direction of the flow too, although lava will usually quickly burn things up.

Lava flows more slowly than water. In the *Minecraft* Overworld and the End, it also doesn't flow as far horizontally, or from side to side. It will travel three blocks horizontally from a source block, although it will travel farther downward.

MINECRAFT MANIA

The Overworld, the Nether, and the End are the three *Minecraft* **dimensions**. The Overworld is the main world where a player starts, with plants, water, and many different biomes.

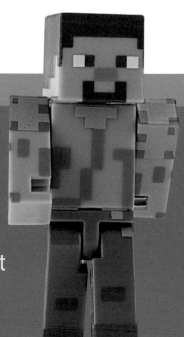

Minecraft lava can turn air blocks around it to fire blocks. Because of this, it can set many things around it on fire, and the fire can spread.

Minecraft water works the same in many ways but a bit differently in others. It will spread seven blocks horizontally from a source block on a flat surface, but it will spread downward as long as it has air blocks to flow into. The farther it spreads outward, the less "full" the block will be.

Blocks can be considered waterlogged in the game. This means that a block of space that has an item in it that doesn't take up the full cube may also hold a water source block. This can include fences, doors, and plants.

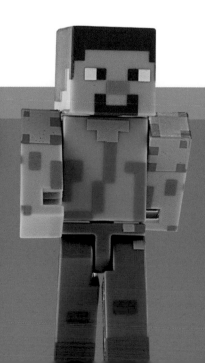

MINECRAFT MANIA

You can create a small water source in *Minecraft* by digging a one-block-deep hole that's two blocks by two blocks wide. Place one bucket of water in each of two opposing corners.

Minecraft has shipwrecks that can be found underwater or all or partly on land. The ones underwater will have waterlogged items like fence posts and chests.

In Motion

Many things in *Minecraft* move, and motion is part of physics. Mobs, which include animals, monsters, and villagers, move on their own. Other things move too, including **vehicles** such as boats and minecarts. Blocks can move with gravity. Weapons such as swords and arrows move when used by a player or mob.

Many of these things can be moved by water. The force from explosions can move some too. Most **entities** in range of an explosion will be propelled, or moved, away from the blast. The closer they are to the blast, and the fewer things there are between them, the faster they'll be moved away.

MINECRAFT MANIA

Real-world explosions cause shock waves. *Minecraft* explosions also have a shock wave effect. Explosions can also cause fires. The damage, or harm, they cause can depend on game settings.

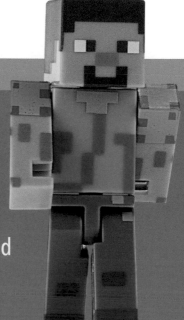

Things in *Minecraft* that can cause explosions include TNT, creepers, charged creepers, fireballs, and withers.

Ways to Move

Motion in *Minecraft* includes forms of **transportation**. By themselves, players can walk, sprint (or run), sneak, swim, and jump. There are also boats, minecarts, and horses (and a few other animals) that a player can ride.

These ways of moving have different speeds. Speed, scientifically speaking, is equal to the distance something travels divided by the time it takes to travel that distance. The fastest way to travel in *Minecraft* (without any **potions** or **enchantments**) is by boat on flat blue ice. A player can move about 72 blocks per second this way. The regular walking speed for a player is about 4.3 blocks per second!

MINECRAFT MANIA

Blue ice generates in frozen ocean biomes, often at the bottom of icebergs. It's more slippery than regular ice, frosted ice, or packed ice.

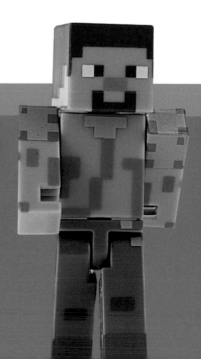

"Terminal velocity" is an idea in physics that means the top speed that can be gained by something falling. *Minecraft* has terminal velocity too. It's about 78 blocks per second for a player! Take care around cliffs.

Light and Heat

Physicists also study light and heat. The study of light is called optics, while the study of heat is called thermodynamics. Understanding how these things work in *Minecraft* can help you. Light affects what you can see, when mobs appear, and how plants grow. Heat affects what biomes generate and if ice melts.

There are 16 possible light levels in *Minecraft*. Light can come from the sun or from some blocks and items. Blocks also let different amounts of light through them. They range from transparent (most light passes through) to opaque (no light passes through). Glass, for example, is transparent. Stone is opaque.

MINECRAFT MANIA

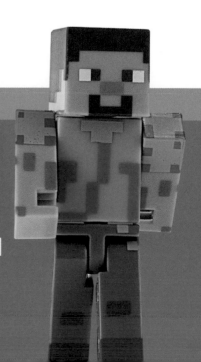

Players are only directly affected by heat in *Minecraft* in two cases: if they are burned by fire or lava or if they freeze after they fall in powder snow.

A potion of night vision gives you a light level of 15 and will let you see in the dark even in huge caves. But be careful it doesn't run out, or you'll be stuck!

Night Vision
Potion

Redstone Power

Matter and electric charges are part of the study of physics. *Minecraft* has its own kind of electrical power. It's carried through redstone dust and used through redstone **circuits**. These can start or control simple machines—or not-so-simple machines! Players have made some amazing things.

Redstone dust works like a wire when you place it on a block. It also is part of many crafting recipes. It can transmit power from sources (such as redstone torches, buttons, or levers) to other components, or parts (such as pistons, redstone lamps, or dispensers). Experiment and see what you can do!

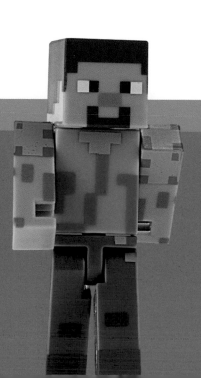

MINECRAFT MANIA

You can get redstone dust by mining redstone ore deep underground. You must use at least an iron pickaxe, and the ore block will drop four or five pieces of dust.

These are a few *Minecraft* items made with redstone. You can build many machines with the right power and circuits.

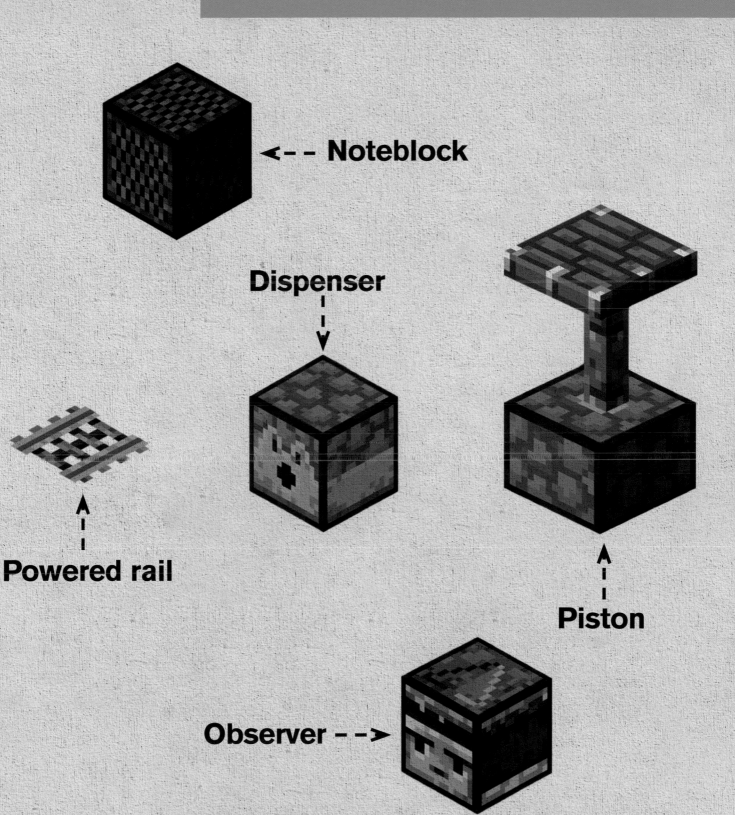

<- - - Noteblock

Dispenser

Powered rail

Piston

Observer - ->

Glossary

anvil: A heavy iron block on which metal is shaped. In *Minecraft*, an item used to repair things, rename items, and combine enchantments.

circuit: The complete path of an electrical current.

dimension: A level of existence.

disturb: To change or upset something.

enchantment: Something that enchants, or affects as if by magic. In *Minecraft*, a way of giving tools and weapons better or extra abilities.

entity: Something that has independent existence. In *Minecraft,* an independently moving object.

fluid: A substance that flows freely like water.

generate: To cause to be created.

lava: Hot, melted rock above the ground.

potion: A drink meant to have a magical effect on someone.

scaffolding: A system of scaffolds, or moveable platforms for workers. In *Minecraft,* a climbable, easy-to-break block.

transportation: A way of traveling from one place to another.

vehicle: A machine used to carry things from one place to another.

For More Information

BOOKS

Baker, Laura. *Physics for Curious Kids.* London, England: Arcturus, 2022.

Colon, Erica L. *Awesome Physics Experiments for Kids.* Emeryville, CA: Rockridge Press, 2019.

Daley, James. *The Science of Minecraft.* New York, NY: Skyhorse Publishing, 2022.

WEBSITES

Minecraft Physics
www.wired.com/2012/02/minecraft-physics/
Wired sets up a physics experiment in *Minecraft*.

Physics for Kids
www.ducksters.com/science/physics/
Duckster takes a look at this branch of science.

What Is Physics?
amnh.org/explore/ology/physics
The American Museum of Natural History offers a ton of kid-friendly physics information and activities.

Index

C
caves, 8

E
End, the, 10
electricity, 20
energy, 4
explosion, 14, 15

F
fire, 11, 14, 18
fluids, 4, 10
force, 4

G
gravel, 8
gravity, 4, 6, 8, 10, 14

H
heat, 18

L
lava, 4, 10, 11, 18
light, 18, 19

M
matter, 4, 20
mobs, 8, 14, 18
motion, 4, 14, 16

N
Nether, the, 10

R
redstone, 20, 21

S
sand, 8, 9
speed, 16, 17

V
vehicles, 14, 16

W
water, 4, 5, 8, 9, 10, 12, 13, 14
waterfalls, 5
weight, 6